WHITELESS THOUGHTS

BITS OF DARKNESS AND LOVE

POEMS

**WRITTEN
BY**

LAVI PICU

WHITELESS THOUGHTS
- BITS OF DARKNESS AND LOVE

Text & Illustrations Copyright © 2017 by Lavi Picu.

ALL RIGHTS RESERVED

Publication date: 2017-05-01
Printed and Bound within USA.

First edition First printing

ISBN:
EBook: 978-0-9959589-0-6
Paperback: 978-0-9959589-1-3

DEDICATION

To my aunt Shyama, who encouraged me to publish my work.

To my family, who has been close to me despite the distance between us.

TABLE OF THOUGHTS

AWAKEN

Everyone has forgotten to smile,
all are trapped in this lie called "*life*"
no one cares if the sun is up on the sky,
no one cares if you live or die.

There is no more time to spend outside,
to feel the wind, or see the grass grow,
to look at the caterpillars march and crawl;
it`s the endless winter of our hearts,
snow, snow, snow...
we became so cruel and cold!

Glimpses of a falling soul, a weakened heart,
are scattered in our moist breath,
reminding of a different life,
when we used to be human.

We`re not departed or possessed,
we`re not ghosts or depressed,
we`re just time oppressed and obsessed...
who`s living our life?

How come we don`t rejoice it`s summer?
`til when we`ll say: "*Tomorrow*!"

I stepped outside and took an oath:
I swore to stay away from the corporate world,
I chose to be an outcast
just to have another chance
to LIVE and LOVE.

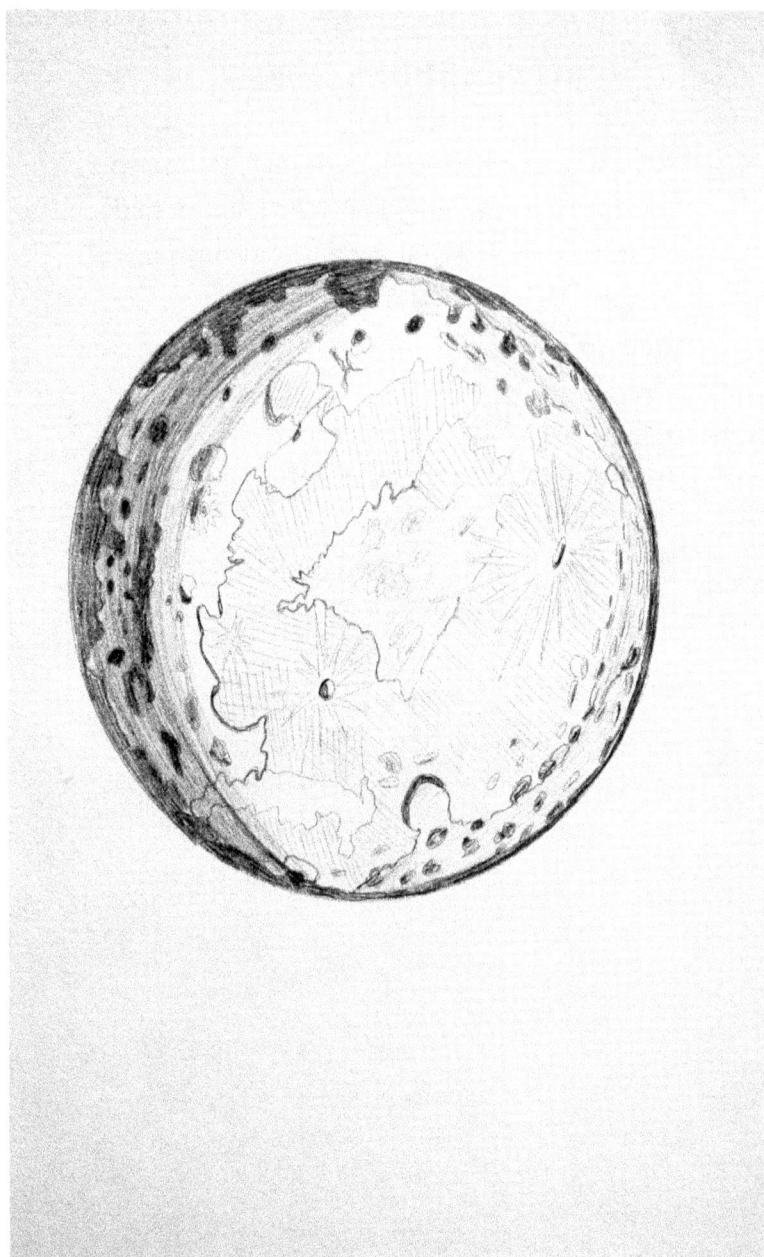

BITTER MOON

Let me have one more look at the bitter moon,
tonight I'll do nothing, stay in bed, linger 'til noon,
close my eyes and shut myself inside my mind,
let the hours fly by 'til stars start to shine,
lend my tears to the sky -let it cry!

Let me scoop again the bucket of thoughts,
stir in the mould and waive endless plots;
it's in my blood, my veins, my genes,
I can't just forget the trouble and pain
or lie to myself this is not who I am.

Let me fall prey to my fifth thought,
follow it through to the end of the path,
thinking of it as the original draft,
shaking down walls and chains off my heart,
reinvent the delightful person I once wrought.

CAGED

On the corner of the cage
I hear some fluttering:
one poor fly has lost a wing
while fighting for its life.

Through the cold dirty bars
something sneaks in and out -
maybe a rat or a nasty thing
I have no name for it.

My eyes no longer see,
my nose has lost the smell,
my lips are cracked as a dried well,
my feet are red and bleeding.

Once in a way the door gets slammed
and then I hear a shiver;
the creatures of the night roam near
while masters drink upstairs wine or beer
and chat about their next (or)deal.

While being caged as an exotic bird
I had enough reflection time;
finally learnt that what I held so dear
costed me nearly twice the price
to have it left unattached.

I still can't believe he sold me
for much less than a dime.

CHAMELEON FACE

Hello Chameleon face!
I know that murky smile upon your face
you kneeled with it whole human race.

They all bowed and kissed your ring,
gave their most precious thing:
their freedom to think.

Forgot everything they learnt in school:
the power to question, tool and rule;
turned the Pope into a fool
in their search for fuel.

We met a while ago, but you couldn't see me
you were so mighty, whereas I
was just plain ME.

We both shared the darkest breath
of the years to come
filled with sorrow, death and regret.

COLD TEARS

Cold tears run down my neck,
feels like that bloody winter
we started fighting over a splinter;
no one to blame but the cold in Quebec!

Morning day light brought delight
meant to last until midnight;
first guest at tonight's feast?
Peter, the sleepy beast!

Lucky bastard!
lustful wishes were unleashed...
is this how they love in Quebec?!
I have to release a signal or I`m gonna break.

COLD WAR

Oceans apart, this one idea grew in my heart
that we should, maybe, share the blame;
move on and be proud of what we got,
understand that we will never be the same.

I put away my pride and called once more;
my mind was saying clearly: "*Not again!*".
I really hoped time had healed my pain,
that I won't hang up at her "*Hello?*".

Her sweet talk gift was no surprise
I still wonder if it was a disguise;
all her lines played in my head
there were not such a big threat.

Those days when I used to play along,
inside me, I knew she was wrong
preaching family, morale and respect-
though one thing she left unchecked:
Love!

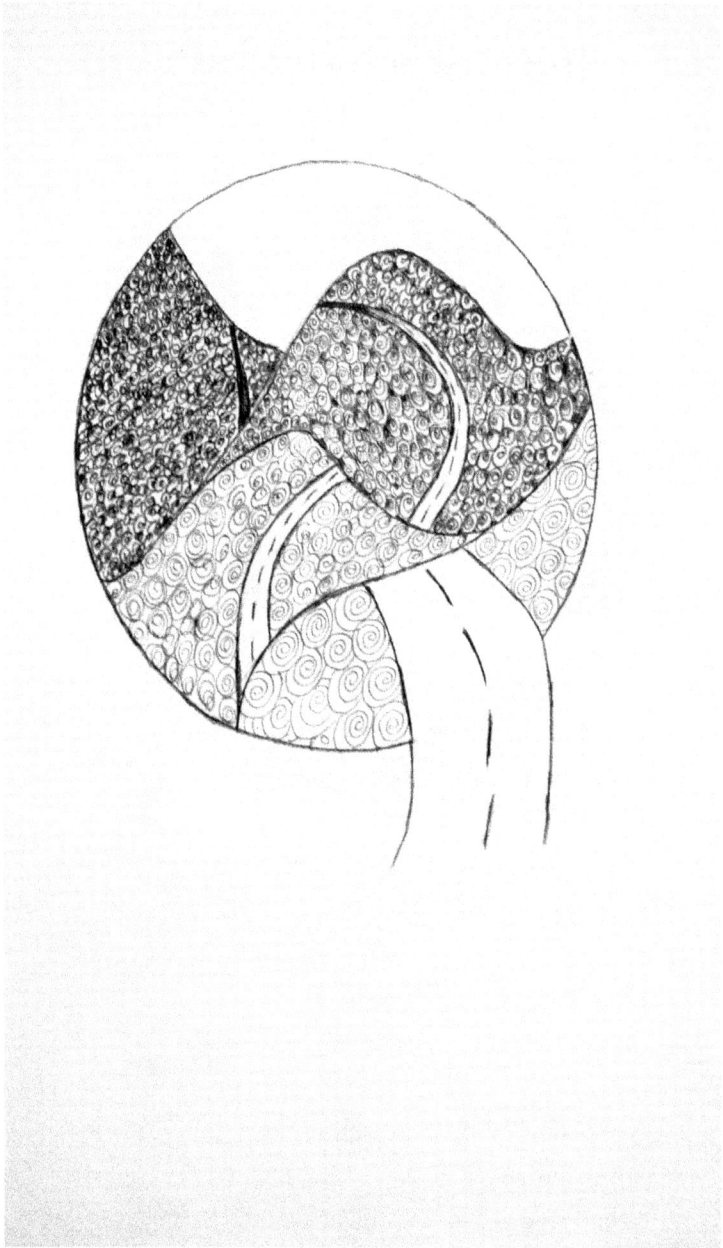

CONFESSION OF THE DAY

I feel the snowflakes
melting on my cheeks,
new memories are built
and confidence is stronger,
an old demon is being burnt
and soon to be forgotten.

I take another sip,
I make another step
I walk alone,
I`m growing older.

My burden is relieved
and though one scar, still red,
is whispering some of my stories.

Who won the battle, you might wonder?
don`t know, don`t care!

I had to let it go,
my soul was getting tired...

Never denied my true self
nor ashamed of it
although one sin will never perish...

CONTEMPORANEITY

People learn about love in poems
some read them as art,
others rip them apart
or maybe search deeper meanings
if they understand their own feelings.

Others play with words and create them,
they let their mind err and turn
random thoughts into immortal wisdom.

Blindfolded with no sense of direction,
I follow the flow
in this river of civilization
where the magnificent trio rules:
money, greed, power.

CRUELLA

I hope you will never get to see
the evil Cruella that lies in me!
I hope, for your own sake,
that none of the feelings was fake!

You never saw this dark side of mine,
you never saw my anger unleashed,
you never saw what I'm capable of,
you never heard me saying:
"F... off!"

DANCE OF THE WOUNDED SOULS

Tell me all your thoughts on God,
when and why you pray or praise,
is there something that you fear?

Have you ever lost your faith?
do you ever question He's unfair?
I just want to know what's real.

The world I know has lost beliefs;
broken hearts, crushed dreams,
pain and sickness on display
spread amid friends, parents, children...

Faith, it's a dance of wounded souls.
Is there anything else?

DARK TIDE

Caught in the rip dark tide
he flowed seaward, hoping to escape,
floating aimlessly into the sea of sins.

The days seemed years,
the years seemed decades,
time fused with his memories.

There was no law or rule,
no guideline or boundaries
in the endless sea.

In the darkness of the night,
offsprings of his wicked mind
slowly, slowly all crawled out.

Mermaids, Circe and Maenads
loved, teased and seized him,
all nursed sins of the flesh.

Countless times he tried
to find the way back
to the place where he had docked.

Wrecked and adrift,
one day he reached
an unknown sandy beach.

DEMON WITHIN

There is a voice in my head
causing me to sin
but don't blame me...
blame the demons within.

Now I fight and I kill,
because soon I'm going to die
believe me, I will...

There won't be tomorrow,
there won't be any sorrow
one more down, just one
and then I'm gonna have to run.

They've ruined my life
stole everything I've got.
now my soul will perish,
because of their plot.

They've caused so much hate
they've caused so much pain
and to them it's all great
that I lost my God and my Faith.

They are feasting now,
having me as their main dish,
they want me to become like them,
a blood-thirsty beast!

To them I'm just a meal;
there is no use to scream
shriek, wail, howl or squeal
I wish it was a bad dream!

I'm locked between these walls,
where no one can hear my calls
I'm waiting now in this cell,
waiting for eternal Hell...

Now... I'm one of them.
now... they are in me.
Look and you will see
a beast with a gem.

Follow the blood in the air,
and come to the lair
they've dragged me in
to shed my skin.

Now I am the first sin.
I am not what I've been,
now I am the demon within!

EMPTY LOVE NEST

It drives me insane to see I'm a prize in this game
why can't you see who I am;
you can't be so indifferent to my pain.

Turn around and see my eyes
before this last tear dries -
you broke all the walls around me,
now you better go and let me be.

Let me crawl out of my misery,
deal with my rage inwardly...
I'm sure there won't be a thing I'd miss,
breathing you out is quite a bliss!

"I tried so much to be a better man
I did all right, but I still failed."

What scares me the most is seeing everything go,
rolling down the road: feelings, whispers, hopes...
there's no love nest without your sweet caress.

FAILING

If I could make a step out of the rain cloud,
I'd do it towards you.
I'd grab your hand and pull to drag you in
just to give you a taste of your own medicine.

I lost the count how many times
you promised something
and never meant a bloody thing.

You had everyone fooled but me
Mr. Clean, I know you for a while...
under your humble clothes and polished smile,
your soul is dark and your words mean.

The holes, the marks, the empty words
have all darkened my heart.
I am afraid one day it'll stop
and it will be because of failure.

I failed you. I failed myself.
I failed so many others...
the thing I regret failing the most
is not failing you earlier.

It would have saved me all this pain,
I would have found myself
longing for the rain...
instead, I am stuck with it forever.

FIGHTING BACK

Tonight I left the bed, I`m on my way!
I walk fast through the dark,
there`s nothing stopping me.
Tonight I took another oath,
left all behind and became master of my path.

I've been away from the road for so long;
no time to waste now. I won`t wait!
This time I'll settle it my own way;
things have changed,
nothing looks the same after dark.

Lyme bent me down, but with a bit of faith
I will walk straight again.
I won`t settle in for it,
I won`t accept it,
I won`t be quiet!

I am taking my life back,
I fight my Lyme,
this is my time!
I own my body
time to take over.

No more denying and feeling sorry;
now I fight back with all the strength left,
I defy tingles, flares and pain
I walk, I herx, I fall and rise again!

No relief in between,
nothing but pain, diet and pills
I gotta make it through.
I have a train to catch,
disregarding your will,
I need to be there on time.

FORGOTTEN

Another lie has been solved,
another truth which was untold
has completed the puzzle.

Was it so hard to say the word?
I forgot who you were...
my eyes don`t know you anymore.

I stitched black ribbons
in the aching part of my heart,
I took you out, you are forgotten.

The mist no longer blinds my sight,
now I could tell wrong from right;
there`s more bitter in my voice,
took me years to rejoice.

Scrambled thoughts and random flashes
everything else turned into ashes.

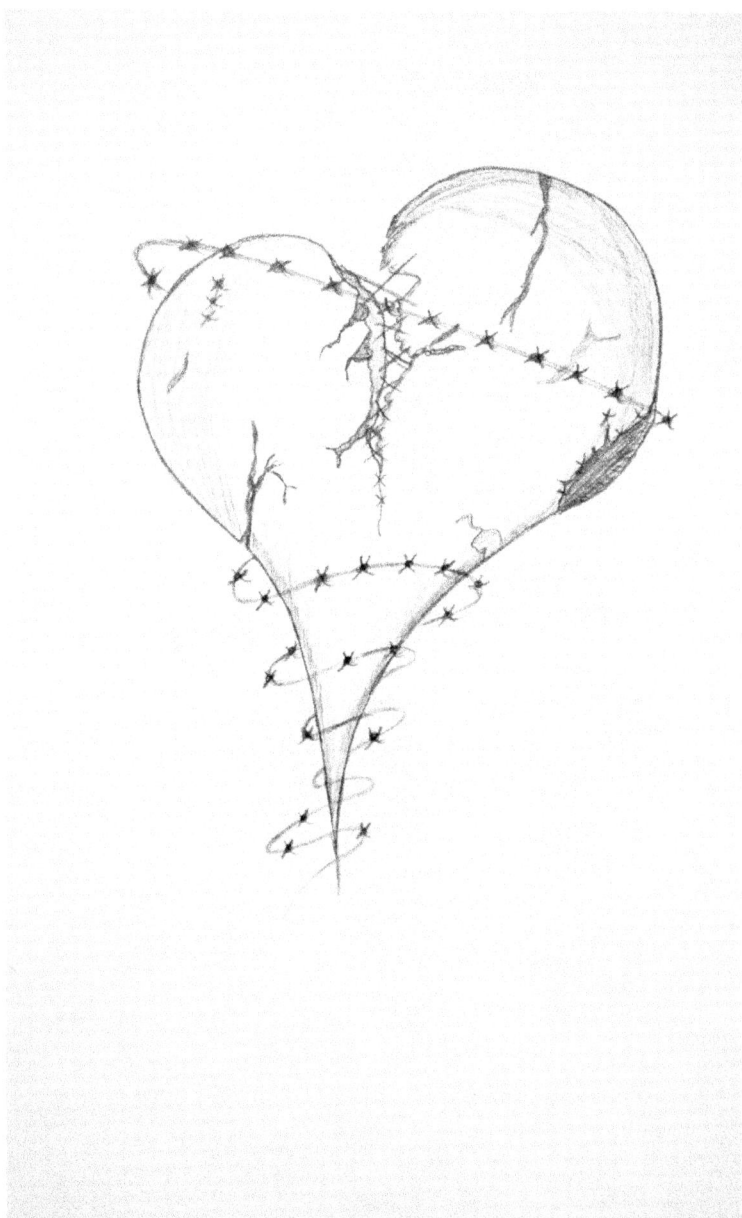

I WONDER

Do all women weep in bed
or is it only me?

Do all men behave like jerks
or is it only you?

Why do you say some things
you never mean to happen?

Why do make a promise
with no intent to keep it?

Why you have to be different
when someone is around?

Why do you choose sides
when there's no gain in this battle?

What makes you think
you're right this time?

Or do you even care?

How am I supposed to cope with it
when you make no f....ing effort?

How can you believe that
this is only my problem?

Why can't you say a word that comforts
instead of being silent?

IRONIC

How great is that each time I think we're fine,
a few seconds later, I find myself left hanging on a
vine?
How come your moods switch faster then the wind,
leaving me speechless and without having any hint
about what the next second may or may not bring.

It used to be fun to hang around with you:
we danced and drank and chat 'til dawn,
we smoke and rolled in the back lawn,
we travelled the world, got bumped in first class,
we buried your shoes, deep under green grass.

But after all the things you put me through
I ask myself if was it worth the ride?
Now you make me wanna run and hide-
how did our galaxies ever collide?

I'm out of words, as broken promises make me choke,
your chameleon skin hides the heart of an old
artichoke:
too many layers to cut and peel off -I'm getting tired!
too many b.s. to listen. I say: "F... off!"

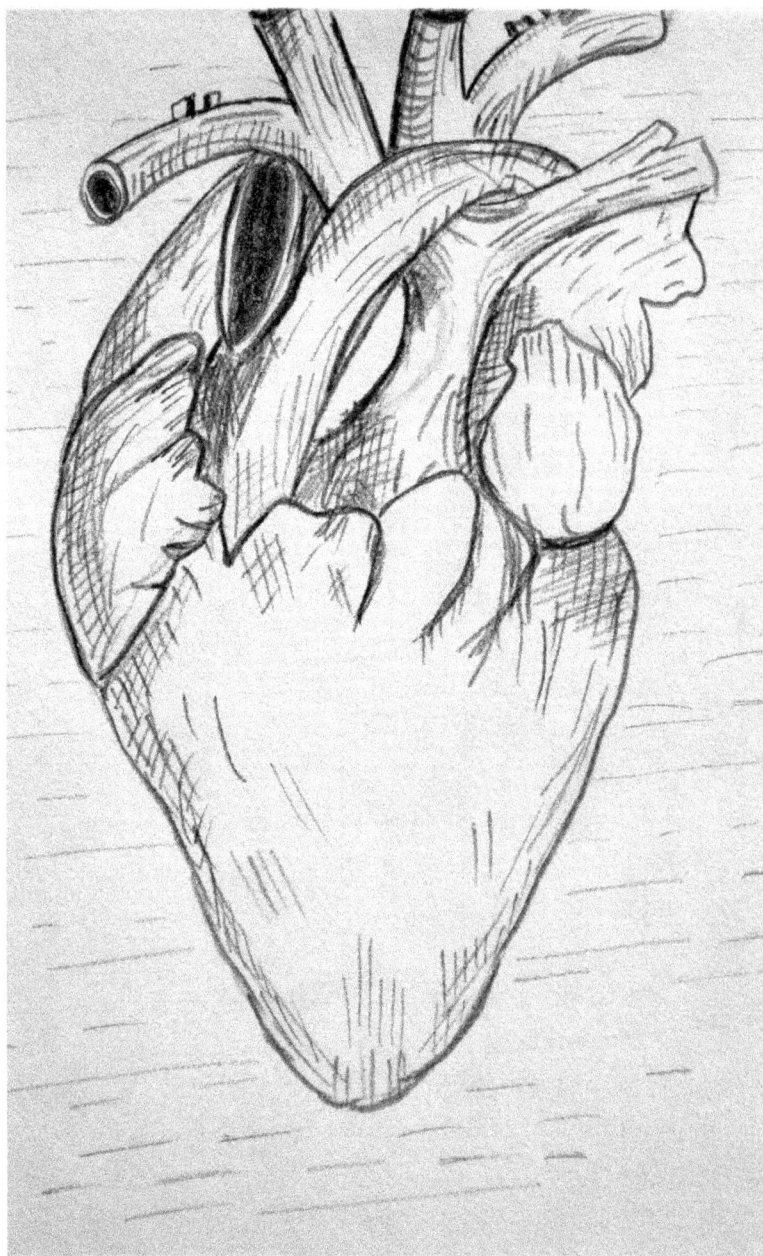

KNOWING

I held my breath as long as I could
stood still, listened to my heart beats
trying to ignore all the noise around
and see you.

How can I translate this into words,
when I can not even say your name
without thinking it might trigger
a negative response.

Feels like mining for fools' gold
with bare hands;
you've always been so far away,
intangible for me.

I did not share this dream with anyone
for fear it could delay or jinx the day
I'd actually meet you.

The world collapsed and we plunged
in the darkness;
for once I admit I am afraid,
but this won't change a thing.

Can`t explain how or what
I just knew you were there,
somewhere around; I always
hoped it would make difference.

LIES

Everything feels off track as if
I've been going in the wrong direction-
did I forget where was I going?

I gave so much, I worked for two,
but still I am invisible!

My golden path turned out
to be a cruel illusion,
as in real life, all I can see
are closed doors and fake smiles.

What was I believing?
I am stuck in this position
there's only one way out:
QUIT!

LONELINESS

Loneliness is not an easy bird,
there's more to it than just a quiet game;
you play along, you cope with it,
you think that you can handle it;
but it always brings much more
than you'd ever asked or imagined.

Loneliness awakes the demons
within your heart and soul-
it takes you back in time,
when you'd surrendered pain,
torments your nights and makes them light.

It's rather like a dormant giant monster:
it teases you when you want more,
it pleases you when you're wrong,
it wraps itself around yourself
to justify its subtle taking over,
it breaks your heart and tames your will,
it tears you up when you're alone,
it dries you up into a raisin.

LONG WAY DOWN 1

You curious boy,
you should have not walked outside
at this late hour of the darkest night.

You curious boy,
you should have not run away,
it could have saved you another day.

You curios boy,
what did you think you would do
when lights are down,
with no one around,
no one to save you...

You curious boy,
you should have not scratched
to catch a glimpse of what hides
under the bloody cloth covering your wounds...

You curious boy,
you should have not peaked
on a place like this,
there is nothing here
you would need or miss.

You curious boy,
your eyes should have not met the pain...
It's a long way down!

You curious boy,
this path was not meant to be yours,
God has mistaken it-
your heart is not able to go through all this!

You curious boy,
I had nothing on my paper for your little soul,
but since you're here, I could take away the pain;
beyond this door there's no flesh, soul or self-control.

LONG WAY DOWN 2

There is something pulling me through that door
I had a glance and there is a long long way down;
for unknown reasons my legs just can't stop.
As much I try to go back
there is a thread pulling me
to the depths of the chambers.
I search each corner looking for the truth
I doubt my decision, how can I know if I am right?

You should have not trusted any stranger
but now there is no turning back.
Let me show you how much I care:
you will never be broke,
you will never go back,
you will never feel down,
you will never be alone.

I'll teach you to master the desire,
to be higher than your inner fire.
Let me shackle you out of your mortal chains,
hoping this chalice will tackle your brains.

Surrender to the darkness!

Each breath you take in makes you mine;
when you exhale and your eyes tear,
the pain brings you closer to the edge-
how do you humans say:
caught between the devil and the sea?

Now you can understand this choice is right;
you know you got no strength to fight.
Why would you? Is there something you will miss?

All those pretty faces have sold you out,
their greed is beyond any doubt;
they took the kiss upon my lips,
the instant you were gone.
Why do you look surprised
when people tell you sweet lies?

Don't waste the time to ask yourself
if there was a turning point-
you know it well, there was none!

It was all in your eyes and mind.
You know you called for me!
There is no way to run from pain
when you are human.

For centuries you have whispered
my name, my refrain..
You called for me and now I'm here!
Surrender!

Read my mind, see through my eyes
what lays ahead: numbing pains,
tingling, tremors, spasms and crippling fears.

Have a look at this bleak summary
of your upcoming years!
Anxious? Any thrills to go through?
So, little boy, are you coming?

MARIPOSA'S SONG

Behind cold bars and closed doors
where you can't tell day from night,
time squeezes seconds into minutes
days into weeks, weeks into years.

Occasionally a match is lit and then
glimpses of casted shadows
leave the walls, come forward
to whistle Mariposa's song,
the Black Witch.

Whispers bring to life a long forgotten story
of an undecided widow, a *"devil in disguise"*,
casted to die by her offended suitors,
whose egos succumbed to their wounded pride.

Her only faults were shattered faith and self-
withdrawn;
nevertheless she was brought to court,
accused of witchcraft and insanity,
charged and looked with jaundiced eyes...
needless to say the judges were unfair.

During the trial she stood still,
gilded in her wedding shroud,
she never spoke, nor looked afraid.

Tears never welled up her eyes,
she seemed absent-minded, far-away;
no one recalled a sight or cry for help.

Some believed she took a silence vow,
others claimed her spirit was on different realms
where she could witness the birth of clouds.

The callous wigs have locked her up,
never again she saw a ray of light-
the stoned wall of her wretched cell
served as her only friend, a quiet listener.

She spend the days living completely in her mind,
seeming unaware of those who tried to gain her trust,
ignoring guards who visited only to saturate their lust
until one day when she disappeared,
leaving behind nothing but a sorrow moth.

Rumours told about devil casting a spell,
allowing her to change shape and transcend
to the realm where she was already half present.

Locals feared she'd return for vengeance,
that she'd entrapped their souls with her venom,
preventing them from reaching God's heaven.

To save their souls, in the nights,
they hunted down butterflies and moths,
burnt them singing gospels and old chants.

MAYBE

Another year went by, and also a not so quite summer,
the clouds are whispering and crying since you left...
you could have changed something,
but you were in a hurry...
You were expected, maybe?!
Don`t wanna know! Don't tell me!

Damn! I had so much to say and offer...
We didn't have the time to say *"Farewell!"*
We never did. I wonder who`s to blame?

You know, at night, in my sleep,
it`s haunting me, and all seems so real!
How could you? What`s left to do?
Lie to myself? No more!!!
All seems to be forgotten
and a cold silence is gaining our souls.

Have you ever really meant it?
Now, I can bet you don`t have a clue
how it feels like deep down inside...

MILES AWAY

So many miles away and still not enough!
I won`t miss this blue,
I don`t wanna go through it again,
I need some space, not a war!

My eyes are crying without tears,
my sympathy reached its limits.
I wish I could see it so simple as you
I wish you could see it as me.

We've been through this before,
talked it all through,
but promises ran cold
and I just can`t move on!

More time I spent inside, less I know you;
this hell ain't mine, and I ain't as selfish as you.
Step outside the bubble and see the truth!
I don`t need you to say I `m right or wrong.

Words are chocking in my throat
and you just shut me out.
You really think you are able
to pass this moment
with a kiss on my back?

Aching
&
aching

Either you like it or not,
this world has some basic rules;
can`t always drift away,
letting things just happen,
won`t help or make it better.

Do you ever think of me?
how it makes me feel?
do you ever search deeper,
or try to understand my reasons?
the world ain't as shallow as your philosophy.

Just keep breathing and going further,
pretending it`s ok, won`t work forever;
all this steaming and cooling
add more scars to my aching heart.

I don`t know how you
see this story go,
but it`s half way
and my bandages broke.

MISCHIEVOUS EYES

I used to think you were a friend,
treated you as my best friend,
I cried and laughed with you so many times,
I listened and kept inside me all your crimes,
I stood beside you and shared your pain
telling you all your fears were in vain.

Close ones warned me about you,
said you weren't true, not to me, not even to you.
Maybe I just didn't want to see it through,
convinced myself I didn't share their view.
I don't understand how you seem to forget
the things I witnessed ever since we've met.

What happened to you my dear friend?
Is it the money scent or that's the latest trend
looking down on people with discontent?
Since when you became so eloquent?
What makes you think you are above,
who or what gave you the shove?

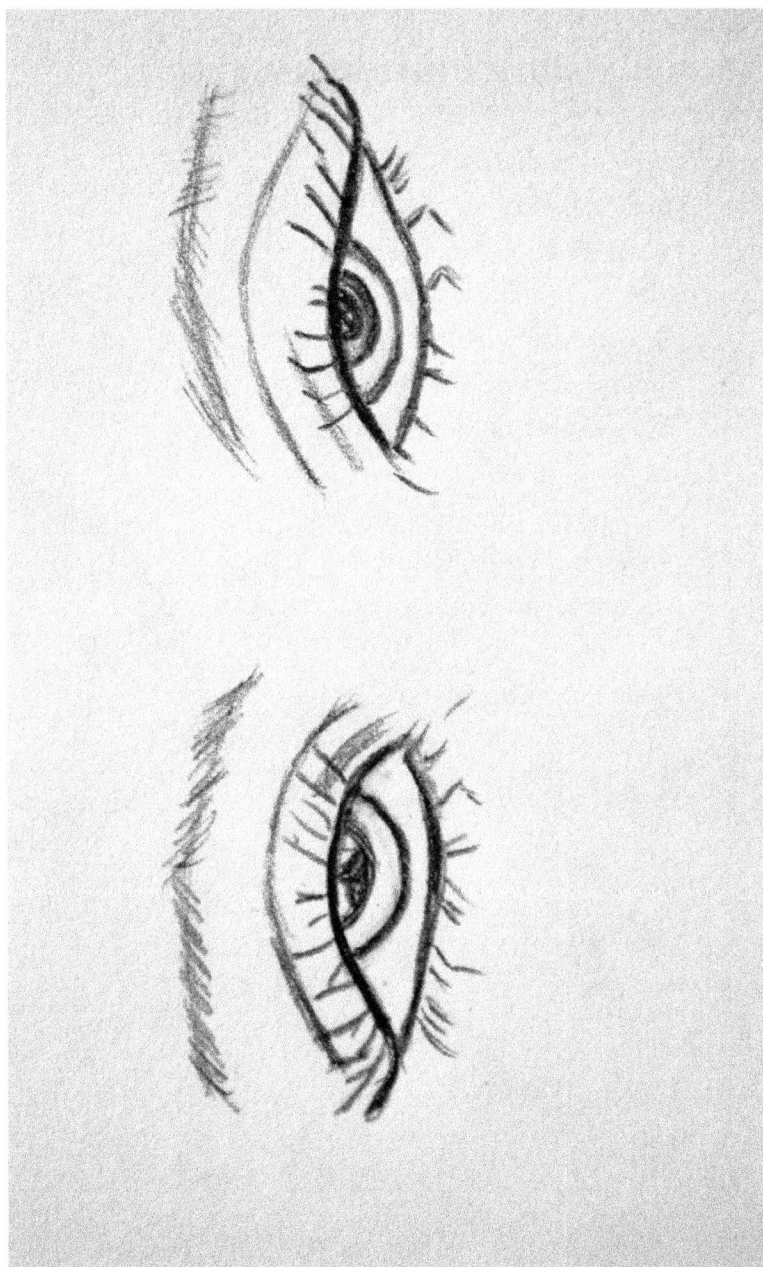

MUSHROOM BURIAL SUIT

Why it's so hard to admit
that one day we get to the moment
when we all die and decay?

Why do we hide behind words
and pretend we are Zen
when there's nothing left in the end?

Prepare my mushroom burial suit
for when I return to dust;
pointless getting fussed!

Lend an ear to good old Johnny Cash:
"There ain't no grave to keep my body down"!

ON THE EDGE

Trapped between the walls I built around me,
a sudden thought urges my escape:
I need to break out; it came the time to hit the road.
The days I have left, I`d rather take it on the edge,
heal my wounds, cry out my rage.

I learnt to cope with pain, we are close friends-
I need to find a way to be myself again,
feel once more the killer spark
before I fall apart and my life ends.

When the day fades out, the crawlers are out
burning under my skin -tingling my veins
there`s no inch left inside me flames did not touch.
It hurts, but I know I`m still alive.
                    I need to break out!

ONENESS

The black cat spoke the truth:
on this page the ink has dried,
nothing to sell, lie, hide or dye.

My heart pumped for Love and
I keep on searching for
the better version of me.

I'm longing for a change,
too many nights spent in denial,
casted in this slave role for quite a while,
the falling darkness swept my tone for centuries
the eyes (chakras) are ready for the never ending ride.

No more secrets and no more lies
can't nurture any of these!
I chewed on my own darkness,
left to prey and feed on my own kind;
now life is fading away with no delay
memories unfolding
on replay...
I die!

Hush!
Get off your knees and stay awake!
Hush!
The mind thinks it's a dream.
Hush!
We are one!

PEANUT

Landed on my knees... Again!
Now, it seemed more like a tease:
put some ice, made it all freeze,
back and forth, without a cease;
would this pain ever ease?

Since you`re not prone to emotional display,
I can`t state he`s led astray...
helplessly, I witness the backwardness
of a peanut in distress.

I don`t care who is to blame,
nor if you feel the same,
or if there is any pain,
guilt, indifference or shame.

You can`t just sympathize!
your role is to strive;
help him find his drive,
be a Shepard in disguise!

Try to feed the dearth of lore,
graze his hunger with more chores!
stonewalling is not the way...
trust me, it won`t make it go away!

PURE VENOM

The morning star misled your path,
it took you an a different part
of the world you once thought
you knew.

I admit, it was my wish to have it so,
therefore, I paid for it, with my own blood.
Now, you're all mine you little swine,
prepare to die!

No squealing please, there is no need for it
in this parts of woods, there's hardly anyone;
besides, who'd care of what happens to a pig
that squeals?

Despite the fact you killed my wife
and drench her in a swine bath,
I will not return the favour.

My ways are different, smoother:
you have a choice between
a black widow or cobra's pure venom.

VENOM

But for now, I'd rather let you long for it.
You know, death comes as a gift;
the truth: there is no escaping.

Before you close your eyes forever
and your last breath it still warm,
you'll see the suffering you caused
To others and to me... as a gift.

Westing too soon won't be enough
to satisfy the thirst for vengeance,
won't take away the pain,
won't bring them back
nor wipe the thousand tears shed.

But you roasting, on the other hand,
hmmm... that sounds quite appealing
the sight of you in vivid flames -
gives you a chance to prove you're brave.

The word has spread that you are near,
the villagers are on their way here,
bringing their axes and pitch forks
as they're anxious to start feasting.

RAIN

On the verge, gasping for air
seeking refuge...
the rain drowns everything tonight;
it washes the trace of your bleeding soles,
more tears ripping your chest

Hang on! Hang on!

Memories and pain, melted by the rain
push you further away
I could never explain...

No strength left to rise up and fight,
your life it was a god damn birthright.

This ain't the true light, little angel
the sorcerers seeded thorns and petals
on your path.

Hang on! Hang on!

RAIN OF THORNS

When I finally unpacked my heart and
thought I left my tears outside the door,
unwilling to suffer more, playing smart,
thinking I finally found the real thing,
I fell asleep feeling alone...

I`m walking through a rain of thorns
you scattered on my way,
I try to follow you
but I keep falling down,
I am running in circles.

My emotions bled tonight...
can`t gravel all out and restart again.
No matter what I say
your convictions stay the same.

Hush! I won`t make a sound...
I saw all the ammo in your eyes

I can`t believe it`s happening to me.

REGRETS

Love, have you ever loved someone,
but they didn't love you?
have you ever felt like crying,
but what good would that do?

Have you ever looked into their eyes,
and said a little prayer?
have you ever looked into their heart,
and wished that you were there?

Don't ever fall in love my friend,
for the price you'll pay is high
if I had to choose between love and death,
I think I'd rather die.

Don't ever fall in love my friend;
you'll get hurt before it's through
you see my friend, I should know
because I fell in love with you.

Regrets? Hmm!... more than a few...

SAUDADE

I met again those eyes, that I once knew,
I saw the sadness within, and prayed I'd be mistaken,
not too much comfort in the words, the grief...
couple of regrets...

I held you tight, and heard your heart beat,
the only proof you're still alive.
The time has left its seeds upon your jolly face,
I saw some white hairs in your beard.

I felt your pain, my dear friend. It hurt so much,
I`d wished to wipe it within seconds.
I'd trade it all again, no second thoughts,
to have that time-window opened,
just to be there, in the end, hand in hand.

For strangers' eyes, it's just a phase... but me,
I know it's going to be there.
In this cruel world, worst of our fears come true;
Each time I close my eyes, I talk to you
so tell me if there's something I could do,
to heal your heart and dry your tears?

SCRAP

I am sick of needles, pokes and pricks
having stings on calves, hands, arms
tired of hearing the naturalist:
"pull this! stretch this! hold this!
do you feel it in your wrist?
take this! try that!
eat these,
lose those!"

The night is coming: shadows and whispers
the Lyme crawlers are having fun.
I can't keep this pain inside,
I surrender!
I am falling apart,
I am total scrap!
Scrap!

SILENCE

The silence usually tells more than it should;
you never know when it started or why,
how long it will last, or who`d put an end to it.

You just feel it there, cooling everything around you,
defying your judgment, staggering,
making you see things like never before.

At the beginning, you ignore it, and play a long
you never know what it'll bring you...
you cope with it although it seems so childish..
you let it grow, you seed the doubts,
and in the end, it takes over.

As far as you know it wasn't you
it couldn't be -not now, or ever!
what happen with *"you had me at hello!"*?

Don`t you know by now that
each unsaid word means a broken promise,
each moment missed takes you a step back,
much further from the moment
where everything depended on a kiss.

The silence usually tells more than it should.
you became immune to it, while I am just invisible.

SILENCE IS COLD

Silence's as cold as the gold,
it doesn't warm you in the night,
wraps around you -it ain't right.

In this silence, your breath is so loud
your thoughts, a war cloud you can't avoid;
it will drag out all the issues you tried to settle before
now you're all drained, you whisper no more...

Who am I to ask you how or why
when you can't even say goodbye...
you have no words to tell me-
that's fine, I know it is not a game.

Thus don't try to lie to me,
tonight you sleep alone,
all silent, in the cold.

SMOKEY EYES
(GOTHIC BEAUTY)

This world is painted in black and white
and everything is spinning fast;
we're caught into a net of lies
with no choice but to comply.

Your tarnished eyes are ravaging my soul,
haunting my dreams and shortening my nights.
I wonder what hides underneath this sad look,
what could have made them so dark grey?

It took me months to understand
your smokey eyes were not a trend
you followed bluntly...
I got it, you are still under the spell.

SPIDER QUEEN

You put your seal, you left your mark,
you wiped the joy out of her heart,
you've seen her in her knees
rolling in and out all sorts of miseries.

Tormented, haunted by sorrow and regrets,
her life, a living hell; trapped in your cobwebs,
wandering around, never giving up,
looking for a sign, always on the run.

She never crossed the line,
condemned to live outside of time,
confined to the dark and murky woods,
being bounded by her old ways roots.

She gained her living by stitching rugs
and feeding on the forest's shrubs;
despite the snarled unbrushed hair,
the scanty pockets, her beauty never disappeared.

She fought demons, thieves, dragons, no exemption;
the shadows of her past dried out her tears,
her chapped lips murmured on and on for years
only one word: redemption... redemption.

Today the deal is done;
she managed to survive
and you had your fun,
you got your satisfaction.

It passed your time, you demon head,
you couldn't break her down;
now lift the spell and walk away,
give her the chance to shine again.

Listen to her song at the brink of day,
the way she strokes the strings,
her finger picks are bleeding,
each pinch reveals parts of her story,
moments of fear, anger or despair...
Undo the curse and walk away!

STILLNESS

Into this world the Gods missed their waking call,
heaven lost its blissful glow, light turned into ashes.

The chaperones' words aren't reaching far,
this old hand scribbles non-sense.

Today the prey and hunter are changing clothes,
no space for wonder in your mind.

Thoughts are no longer roaming freely,
the voices in your head are never answered.

Walls have ears when living in a world ruled by fear,
doors are all closed and gold became the master key.

Misleading steps and howling truths
pushed you so close to westing.

Once you passed the fog of thoughts,
you embraced the void, its aching emptiness.

You walked these bones and chewed your grief
beyond the point where all wants ceased,

Outside the time and silence, where you forgot
about the trace of blood upon your hands.

A new day and dawn spring within you
while harvest of the soul is done in stillness,

Your endless quest for the breath of God
ends where the dance of nature started.

Everything springs from within.

THE DAY

Why do we always choose to celebrate
The Day, as if there's none to follow?
why do we love to cherish past events
instead of looking forward?

What makes it so distinct for us to treasure
that damn second when everything went wrong?
It's stuck, embedded in our minds forever.

We pride ourselves that we have learnt a lesson:
avoidance, caution, guidance -which one was it key,
you name it -whatever suits you best.

Why do we like to revel in defeats and shameful
stories?
Gone are the times when sadnesses were sobbed in
privacy and silence,
now we post online the grief in our search of solace.

Why do we easily forget the laughs and joys
but never stop trumpeting our sorrows?
We never cease to linger,
we seem unable to overcome the past
which hold us captives;
being miserable, it's in our human nature.

THE END

Tired of meaningless perfect days,
of living somebody else's life,
I packed the sorrows, cauterized the wounds...
The end.

I burnt a bridge... no farewell, no goodbyes,
not even one fake promise of a word,
the time had come to turn the page.
The end.

In a summer cloudless day
I told the truth, I felt the edge
I couldn't take it anymore.
The end.

The life went on, time didn't stop
despite my anger or my pain.
It was a shock! I lost and found myself within a day.
The end.

That day I promised myself
no one would ever break me down;
the bubble burst.
The end.

How many times you tried
to help me while I was down?
None.

How much you really cared
while I was fighting for my life?
That was the death of a dream.

I had to figure the rest of my life
living among strangers,
decide who I really was.

This time, there will be no rules,
no have to-s or conventions;
this isn't a kibbutz!

I kept my silent distance for twelve seasons
never looked back on that track,
I sought to snub the thought
we shared the same blood.

THE NEW WORLD

My soul's unfed, tonight I lost my fear
nothing but violence and destruction on TV
beneath masks I peek illusions of glamour or beauty
smoke and mirrors, all mastered by tiny 'lil lizzie feet.

Feels weird being in my so called *real shoes*
Oh! we're supposed to be strong, unequaled,
but we're all lured by power and control;
no one cares: no friends, no family, no lover
the new trend is: "*It's all about ME! ME! ME!*"

All dreams come labeled as "*fulfill your destiny*",
in this world even God battles for his title of deity;
the whole race forgot its rightful place and
ended in its knees well before the end of century.

THE SOUND OF SILENCE

The sound of silence
took over my house
since you are gone.

The sound is so loud
is pressing my chest,
aching my heart.

A candle shapes white walls,
floors creak without motion
my pulse is so weak...
everything turned bleak.

I wish I could have said
the magic words and
have my wish granted.

Instead I am starring at the walls
imagining what could have been...
Why did you have to go
so soon to heaven?

THE TRUTH

For those who never saw the truth about this world,
crying for help, with no one to hear their hurl,
how much could a human's heart take,
again and again and again?
        I have only my tears to soften their pain.

To those who never saw the dark face of human kind
whose acts are far beyond atrocious, covered by lies,
hiding unimaginable things, tortures I can`t describe,
        I say you are not blind, open your eyes!

To those who never saw their dreams crushed
nor felt the burden of fighting against time
and lived their youths, lives, partners in crime,
        I say you have been brainwashed!

To those whose obedience and faith were tested,
who renewed their vows fearing they`d be arrested
or demonized and exorcized in the name of God,
        you were left to die there, sitting on your tod!

For those who joined the order and sworn an oath
there is nothing more to be concealed, no doubt
they've seen it all! They all cried loud
once they understood they were the scapegoat.

They've seen their world shattered into pieces
the smell of death's deeply embedded in their breath;
once the veil upon their faces was lifted up
they'd known what was real and what was made up.

Their children's ashes blown in the wind,
the sorrow they could never rewind,
painful memories buried in their mind
still remind them of those left behind.

UNDER MY SKIN

Under my skin there is a war
fought most likely against protozoas.
Night and day, they march restlessly,
making me feel as being on ecstasy:
numbing pain and burning twitches
remind me of ancient witches.

Here I am, empty pockets, not a dime,
spent it all on pills for Lyme!
Had to quit all sweets, smokes and wine,
pay attention to when or what I dine.
My world was so so fine without Lyme,
the only culprit for this crime.

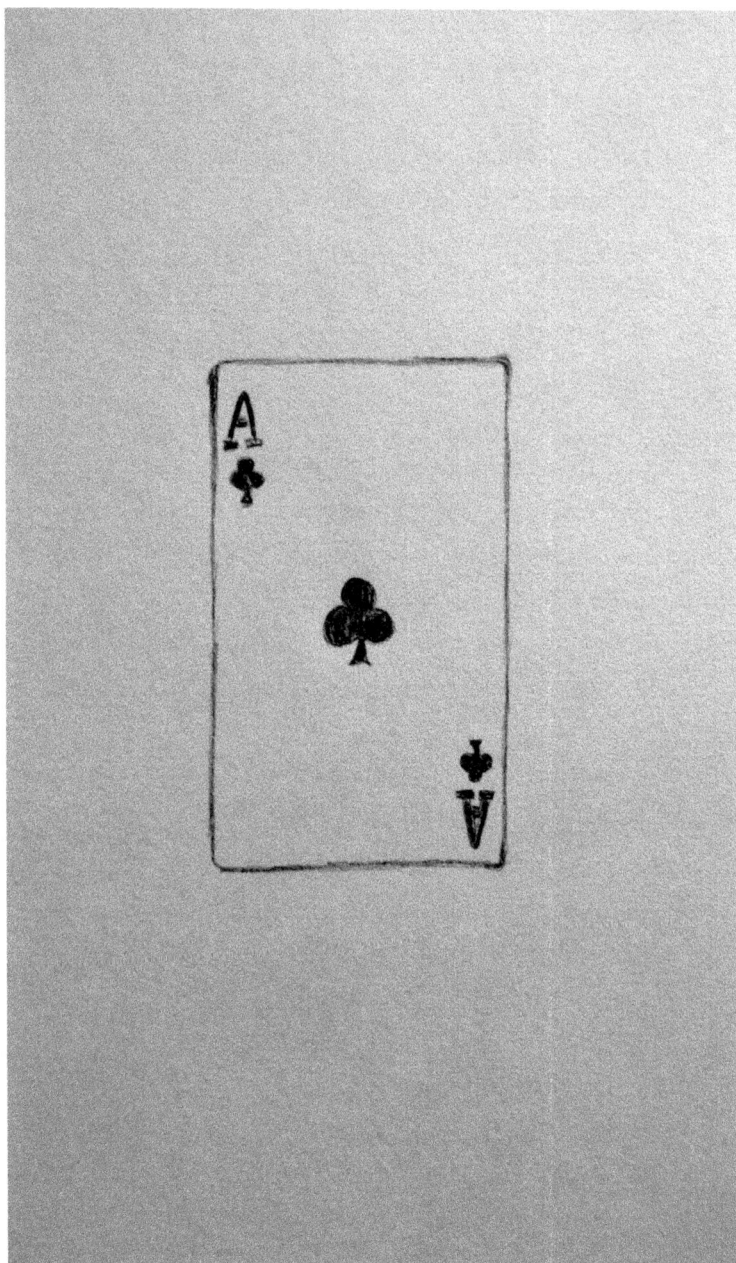

UNFORTUNATE PLAYER

The foundation can not cover anymore
the burden witnessed by his eyes,
the secret is no longer kept;
he truly thought, that in the end,
everything dies...
Except the vice!

Two steps away, in total silence,
a wicked trick was then performed:
a weakened mind fell under the spell,
an easy pray with no defence,
no one around, to hear the poor man yell.
Escape the devil? There`s no chance!!!

At the beginning, pushed by greed,
having more than four mouths to feed,
he built, bid and sold at higher price,
his home, his wife, his sons, his life...
Everything went on the dice.

He tried and tried to keep it straight
he rose and failed several times
eventually, he lost his faith,
that`s when he played for dimes,
agreed to all kind of crimes.

UNREACHEABLE, UNSTOPPABLE YOU

You drive me mad
you lost your mind,
I try to speak
but I can't find
words to better define
the craziness of your
so called...request.

But you, you'd think:
"Hey, sky is the limit!
Let's give poor you
another chance!"

I' m still in shock
all puzzled to see
how easy was and is
for you to lose your soul.

You broke a promise.
and another one right after;
no matter what I have to say
you still don't give a damn.

The only one to blame is me
or my insanity -it made me linger near.
Because of me and my mistakes
an angel's face is frowning now,
wondering why am I in tears.

Damn you and your selfishness,
damn me for being such a fool
to think that you'd learn to care.

You had to blow it all. Again!
Just because you had an itch...
It's hard to keep fighting for the team
when you agreed to let it go
for something worth less than a buck.
Oh, how I wish everything was a bad dream!

Why on Earth I had to fall in love with you?
You broke my heart again in two! Damn you!
I thought I understood your crazy ways
It turns that I was wrong
I can't shut up for every little thing
I am getting tired
And I'm old!
Too old!

ZEN

You fuelled me up and then you're gone,
you dropped the bomb and disappeared;
how could you believe that things
would ever be the same?
The war is done, you lost and
by the way, you're not welcome here!

What is the point to cry about it
when there is no ear around to hear,
no one around to wipe a single tear?

Only a fool could still believe
that after all these years,
you'd change your ways
or treasure my tears.

Long time ago, when I was down
you told me not to be afraid;
now I hit rock bottom,
laying on the ground.

This sordid game came to an end
without a win, I reckon,
from now on, no tears shed, no threats,
no more being second.

A NOTE FROM LAVI PICU

Thank you so much for reading *Whiteless Thoughts – Bits of darkness and Love.* If you enjoyed reading it, please take a moment and leave a short review at your favourite online retailer Amazon USA, CA or EU.

I welcome contact with readers. Check out my author page on Facebook in order to have a sneak peek into my latest poetry projects and leave me a comment. I'd love to hear your thoughts.

At my website www.a-zlyme.com, you can contact me, read my blog and learn a thing or two about Lyme disease.

Lavi Picu

www.ingramcontent.com/pod-product-compliance
Lightning Source LLC
Chambersburg PA
CBHW062007040426
42447CB00010B/1961